IT'S NOT YOUR LEG SON...

THE BOOK OF
SHANKLY

THE WIT AND WISDOM OF
A PEOPLE'S MAN

❝ Correction, it's not your leg son. It's Liverpool's leg.**❞**

To Tommy Smith who was complaining of a leg injury.

Publishers: Steve Faragher, Richard Jones

Editors: Richard Jones, Gideon Kibblewhite

Design: Joe Burt

ISBN 0-9544177-4-7
The first moral right of the author has been asserted.

First published in Great Britain in 2005 by
Naked Guides Limited, 3 Monmouth Place, Bath BA1 2AT.

Front cover picture supplied by Colorsport.
Title page picture: Shankly celebrates winning the First Division Chamionship in 1973,
supplied by Empics.

Collected by **Alex Murphy**

This book is dedicated to the memory of
Bill Shankly (1913-1981)

Contents

Bill Shankly's Career Statistics

Born: Glenbuck, Ayrshire, 2nd September 1913
Died: Broadgreen Hospital, Liverpool, 29th September 1981

As a player

Club	Year	Appearances	Goals
Carlisle	1932	16	0
Preston North End	1933-49	297	13
Scotland	1938-39	5	0
Total		**318**	**13**

Playing honours
1934 Second Division runners-up (with Preston North End) ; 1937 FA Cup finalist (with Preston);
1938 FA Cup winner (with Preston North End)

Scotland appearances
1938 England 0 Scotland 1; Northern Ire 0 Scotland 2; Scotland 3 Wales 2; Scotland 3 Hungary 1.
1939 Scotland 1 England 2. He played a further seven times for Scotland during World War Two.

As a manager*

Club	Year	Games	Won	Lost	Drawn
Carlisle United	1949-51	95	42	22	31
Grimsby Town	1951-53	108	62	25	21
Workington	1954-55	85	35	23	27
Huddersfield T	1955-59	129	49	33	47
Liverpool	1959-74	609	319	152	138
Total		**1026**	**507**	**255**	**264**

Club honours

LIVERPOOL

1962: Second Division champions

1964: First Division champions

1965: FA Cup Winners, European Champions' Cup semi-finalists.

1966: First Division champions, European Cup Winners Cup beaten finalists.

1969: First Division runners-up.

1971: FA Cup beaten finalists, Inter-Cities Fairs Cup semi-finalists.

1973: First Division champions, UEFA Cup winners.

1974: FA Cup winners, First division runners-up Fotball League Division Two champions

*Statistics are for League games only.

THE BOOK OF SHANKLY

OTHER MANAGERS have won more trophies than Shankly, and they are respected and admired for their achievements. The likes of Ramsey, Ferguson and Paisley will live forever in the annals of football for all their World and European Cups. Yet Shankly, a humble son of Ayrshire, earned something more precious than silver: he won the undying love of millions. It is hard to imagine another person whose epitaph is etched into the hearts of so many.

He carved out his unique claim to posterity by transforming Liverpool from a failing Second Division club into one of the world's most august sporting institutions. More than that, he made the club synonymous with its supporters, and forged an unbreakable bond between the men on the field and the fans on the terraces. As the Sixties got underway it proved an unbeatable combination, as Liverpool won promotion to the First Division, added the Championship twice, and the first FA Cup in the club's history. The spirit of Shankly's first great team reflected the vibrancy of the city of Liverpool itself, as the world tapped its feet to the Merseybeat, and the planet tuned in to the sounds of The Beatles. For the first time in decades the docks were full of ships, and the city had a team it could be proud of.

Shankly was not idolised solely for the success he brought to the club. The fiercely proud Scot won the hearts of his adopted city with his warmth, honesty and humour. He also had an unfathomable knowledge of football – he knew players, and he knew how football teams worked. After his first great side of the Sixties began to fade, he had the vision to build up a second great team, which climbed back to the summit of English football.

Shankly retired from the job he loved in 1974, but he handed a rich legacy to his successor, Bob Paisley. When the Reds' first four European Cups followed in the late 1970s and 1980s, Liverpool supporters recalled the debt they owed to Shankly's hard work.

He died too soon in 1981. The city of Liverpool led the mourning, but by now the name of Shankly was revered the football world over, and tributes poured in from every country where the game is played. The boy from the tiny west of Scotland pit village of Glenbuck had made his mark. For all the honours he earned in the game, Shankly did not die a rich man. But you cannot reckon the worth of a man such as Shankly in pounds and pence. He took nothing from the game, and gave it everything.

The simple words on his monument at Anfield neatly sum up why he is still held in such esteem: 'He made the people happy'.

Alex Murphy

THE BEAUTIFUL GAME

Picture: *Shankly at Deepdale in 1937, the year Preston reached the FA Cup Final. He was Man of the Match when Preston won the Cup in 1938. (Empics)*

SIMPLICITY

" Football is a simple game based on the giving and taking of passes, of controlling the ball and of making yourself available to receive a pass. It is terribly simple. "

" Every player in my team has to play for the team not himself. Here we do things collectively. We have specialist players in specialist positions. We don't complicate them so that each player has a simple job to do. "

MIND GAMES

❝ Listen son, you haven't broken your leg. It's all in the mind. ❞
To a player who claimed to have fractured a limb in the Liverpool cause.

❝ We're not too fond of coaching. Coaxing is a better word. ❞
From Shanks – The Authorised Biography.

❝ Forget your strengths. Work on your weaknesses. ❞

❝ If he had gunpowder for brains he couldn't blow his cap off. ❞
Shankly's vivid description of a slow-witted 1970s defender.

PHILOSOPHY

" Anything that a man is is inborn. If he's a football man he's born with that in him… Nobody makes players except mothers and fathers. Not coaches. Time matures players but it does not make them. **"**

" Football is a form of socialism. **"**

TRAINING

" I don't believe in training twice a day. Does them no good at all. We train hard but sensibly. We train for football, little two minutes of torture, half a minute off, then on again. **"**

Quoted in Shanks – The Authorised Biography.

" It's a ninety minute game. But I used to train for a 180-minute game so when the whistle blew at the end I could have played the game all over again. **"**

SEX

“ Too many luxuries can make a man as soft as mush. Overeating and oversleeping can be just as bad as too much drink, too many cigarettes, too many late nights and too much sex. ”

From Shankly, his 1977 autobiography.

“ Footballers are bound to attract women because they are young and fit and famous. Players are virile and alive, and sex in moderation does them good. ”

From Shankly, his 1977 autobiography.

TACTICS

❝ Don't let any goals in. I don't care if we don't score any, I don't want to let any in. That way we'll get 42 points and we won't be relegated. You can add the frills later. **❞**

To Tommy Smith before the 1970/71 season, as Shankly rebuilds his team from the back.

❝ It's better to have a bad system than no system at all. **❞**

❝ Just go out and drop a few hand grenades, son. **❞**

To Kevin Keegan.

MORE PHILOSOPHY

❝ It's the greatest thing in the world, natural enthusiasm. You're nothing without it. ❞

❝ Great to be alive, boys. All you need is the green grass and a ball. ❞

To Liverpool players at the Melwood training ground

❝ An athlete should look like an athlete. His eyes should sparkle so much you could light your cigarette from them. **❞**

From Shankly, his 1977 autobiography.

RIPOSTES

" Aye, so was Douglas Bader and he had a wooden leg. **"**

To Tommy Docherty who had remarked that Tony Hateley was good in the air.

" If it's gold, I'm a 28. **"**

To Bob Paisley on hearing that Adidas wanted to know his shoe size to present him with a golden boot.

SUCCESS

❝ A lot of football success is in the mind. You must believe you are the best and then make sure you are. **❞**

WINNING

AND

LOSING

Picture: *Liverpool players celebrate with Shankly after thrashing Arsenal 5-0 in April 1964 to win the First Division Championship. (Colorsport)*

DESPAIR & ELATION

66 As the ball went home like a bullet, the swish and ripple of the soaking net made a sound that frightened me. 'Pick that one out!' said Lawton, and it was like a knife going through me. 99

Shankly recalls Tommy Lawton's winning goal for England against Scotland in 1939.

66 Nonsense. I've kicked every ball, headed out every cross. I once scored a hat-trick. One was lucky, but the others were great goals. 99

Shankly's reply to a reporter who pointed out he had never played in a derby game.

AUTHORITY

" Christ son, you don't open your mouth for four years, and when you do it's a bloody lie. **"**

After Liverpool's quiet right-back, Chris Lawler, awarded a penalty against Shankly's team in a practice match.

" The trouble with referees is they know the rules, but they don't know the game. **"**

" If a player isn't interfering with play or seeking to gain an advantage, then he should be. **"**

COMMITMENT

" If you are first you are first. If you are second you are nothing. **"**

" He's got a heart the size of a caraway seed. **"**

On an unnamed player he sold.

66 The trouble with you son is that all your brains are in your head. **99**

To an unnamed Liverpool player in the 1960s.

66 You may be right, but it hasn't reached his legs yet. **99**

Shankly's retort to a scout who told him a trialist had 'football in his blood'.

VICTORY

" When the whistle blows at Wembley and you've played in a final you've won, that's the greatest thrill of your life. **"**

*Man of the Match Shankly on winning the 1938 FA Cup final,
Preston North End 1 Huddersfield Town 0.*

PROMOTION

“ We got promotion, but you don't think that is satisfactory do you? Next time we come back for presents we will have won the big league. The First Division. **”**

After Liverpool's board gave each of the players a cigarette case for winning promotion to the First Division in 1962.

" It's the biggest travesty of justice in football history. The score should have been 14-2. **"**

After Liverpool had lost 2-1 to Swansea Town in an FA Cup tie.

" They're nothing but rubbish. Three breakaways, that's all they got. **"**

Shankly puts a brave face on a 3-0 defeat.

RESULTS

❝ We absolutely annihilated England. It was a massacre.
We beat them 5-4. ❞

*Scotland thrashed England at Hampden Park in a wartime international, April 18, 1942.
Shankly scored the winner.*

❝ The best side drew. ❞

After Liverpool had drawn a game 1-1.

❝ I assure you Liverpool will win at home before the season is over. ❞

*At the start of the 1963/64 season, Liverpool lost their first three home matches.
They won their next game at Anfield 6-0 v Wolves and ended as Champions.*

RIVALS

" There's Manchester United and Manchester City at the bottom of Division One, and by God they'll take some shifting. **"**

Shankly relishes a poor season for the Manchester clubs.

" I always look in the paper to see how Everton are doing in the league table – starting from the bottom, of course. **"**

PRIORITIES

❝ Football's not a matter of life and death.
It's much more important than that. **❞**

❝ Sickness would not have kept me away from this one.
If I'd been dead I'd have had them bring my coffin to the
ground, prop it up in the stand and cut a hole in the lid. **❞**

After the Reds beat Everton in the 1971 FA Cup semi-finals.

OTHER PEOPLE

Picture: *Shankly and Jock Stein in the depths of Anfield before Liverpool's 1966 European Cup-Winners' Cup Second Leg against Celtic. (Empics)*

JOCK STEIN

❝ Do you want your share of the gate money,
or shall we return the empties? **❞**

*To Jock Stein, after Celtic played a Cup-Winners' Cup tie at Anfield, and the groundstaff
swept hundreds of empty whisky bottles off the away terraces.*

❝ He trains them the right way, and he gets them to do
what they can do well. He merges them all together. They're all
helping each other. It's a form of socialism without the politics. **❞**

On Jock Stein.

DIXIE DEAN

❝ Now while this is a sad occasion, I think Dixie would have been amazed to know that even in death he could draw a bigger crowd than Everton on a Saturday afternoon. **❞**

At the funeral of Everton legend Dixie Dean.

DIRECTORS

" At a football club, there's a holy trinity – the players, the manager and the supporters. Directors don't come into it. They are only there to sign the cheques, not to make them out. We'll do that, they just sign them. **"**

BRIAN CLOUGH

❝ That man scored 200 goals in 270 matches – an incredible record. And he has won cup after cup as a manager. When he talks, pin back your ears. **❞**

On Brian Clough

❝ Brian Clough's worse than the rain in Manchester. At least God stops that occasionally. **❞**

On Clough again

NOTTINGHAM FOREST

❝ I don't think the people of Nottingham deserve football. It should be taken off them. **❞**

After Forest won the title and two European Cups and still couldn't fill the City Ground.

BILL NICHOLSON

" I see you haven't a match this week, Bill. **"**

To Tottenham manager Bill Nicholson, the week Spurs played Norwich City in the 1973 League Cup Final.

TOMMY DOCHERTY

66 Aye, and I'm one of the 100,000. **99**

To Tommy Docherty, who had boasted that 100,000 would not buy one of his Manchester United players.

LOU MACARI

❝ He couldn't play anyway. I only wanted him for the reserves. **❞**

On Lou Macari, who turned down Shankly to join Manchester United.

EVERTON FC

“ Aye, Everton. **”**

To a barber, who made the mistake of asking Shankly if he wanted anything off the top at a time when the Toffees were leading the First Division.

“ If Everton were playing down the bottom of my garden, I'd draw the curtains. **”**

EMLYN HUGHES

“ Don't you recognise him? That man is the future captain of England. **”**

To a traffic policeman who had stopped him on his way back to Liverpool with his new £65,000 signing from Blackpool.

DENIS LAW

“ Law at 15 was like a little whippet. And when he got the hare he shook it well. He had eyes in the back of his head like Finney had. Guts and ability and determination. He had the lot. ”

On Denis Law, the player he signed as a teenager for Huddersfield Town.

“ Denis Law could dance on eggshells. ”

IAN ST JOHN

66 He's not just the best centre-forward in Britain. He's the only one. **99**

On Ian St John.

---

66 Son, you'll do well here as long as you remember two things. Don't over-eat and don't lose your accent. **99**

Shankly's message to Ian St John when he signed for Liverpool.

---

66 If you're not sure what to do with the ball, just pop it in the net and we'll discuss your options afterwards. **99**

To Ian St John.

IAN CALLAGHAN

❝ He typifies everything that is good in football, and he has never changed. You could stake your life on Ian. ❞

On Ian Callaghan.

TOM FINNEY

❝ When I told people in Scotland that England were coming up with a winger who was better than Matthews they all laughed at me. They weren't laughing when big Geordie Young was running all over Hampden Park looking for Tommy Finney. ❞

❝ You could be right. Mind you Tom's 57. ❞

Shankly's rejoinder after a reporter suggested that Sheffield United's Tony Currie was as good as Finney.

❝ Tommy was grizzly strong and could run for a week. I'd have played him in his overcoat. ❞

On Finney.

ROGER HUNT

❝ He misses a few, but he gets in the right places to miss them. **❞**

On Liverpool centre-forward, Roger Hunt, 1966.

RON YEATS

" He's a colossus. Come outside and I'll give you a walk round him. **"**

" With him at centre-half we could play Arthur Askey in goal. **"**

*Introducing Liverpool's strapping new centre-half, Ron Yeats,
to the Press in 1961.*

" Jesus Christ son, you look eight feet tall. **"**

*To Ron Yeats after the huge centre-half wore Liverpool's
new all-red kit for the first time.*

TOMMY SMITH

❝ You could start a riot in a graveyard. **❞**

To Tommy Smith.

❝ If he isn't named Footballer of the Year, football should be stopped and the men who picked any other player should be sent to the Kremlin. **❞**

On Tommy Smith.

ALAN BALL

" Congratulations son. You'll be playing near a great side. **"**

To Alan Ball, after he joined Everton.

MATT BUSBY

" Why? Is Matt Busby packing it in at Manchester United? "

After Liverpool chairman Tom Williams asked the-then Huddersfield Town manager in 1959 if he wanted to move to the best club in England.

RAY CLEMENCE

❝ Wrong, it's your mother who should have! **❞**

To Ray Clemence who told Shankly 'I should have kept my legs shut' after letting in a fluke goal between his legs.

Picture: *Shankly in his office at Anfield towards the end of the 1968/69 season. (Peter Robinson/Empics)*

THE MANAGER

" I was the best manager in Britain because I was never devious or cheated anyone. I'd break my wife's legs if I played against her, but I'd never cheat her. **"**

" My life is my work. My work is my life. **"**

" Candidly, ladies and gentlemen, I'd much rather be off watching a good football match than sitting here. "

Judging a beauty contest in Carlisle, recorded in Shanks – The Authorised Biography.

HUMANISM

" I was only in the game for the love of football, and I wanted to bring back happiness to the people of Liverpool. **"**

" I'm a people's man, a players' man. You could call me a humanist. **"**

EDUCATION

" Me having no education, I had to use my brains. **"**

CONFRONTATION

❝ Just tell them I completely disagree with everything they say. **❞**

Shankly's instructions to an interpreter at a press conference with Italian journalists.

❝ Why don't you go and jump in the lake? **❞**

To the late BBC Radio Merseyside journalist, Bob Azurdia, who had asked why Liverpool's unbeaten run had ended.

" I can't see you, but I know you're listening. **"**

Shankly standing on a chair talking to a lightbulb somewhere in eastern Europe, convinced his hotel room was bugged.

“ But that's where I live. **”**

*Shankly to a Belgian hotel receptionist who told him he could not put down
'Anfield' as his home address.*

IN CHARGE

" I don't drop players. I make changes. **"**

" The end of the season. **"**

To a reporter who asked him his least-favourite part of football.

❝ I never touch the stuff. I'll donate one to the police raffle and use the other for embrocations. **❞**

After winning gallons of whisky as Manager of the Month in September and October 1972.

RETIREMENT

&& This is not a decision that was taken quickly. It has been on my mind over the last twelve months and I feel it is time I took a rest from the game I have served for 43 years. My wife and I both felt we wanted to have a rest and charge up my batteries again. **&&**

Standing down from the Liverpool job, 12 July 1974.

MARRIAGE

" I've been so wedded to Liverpool that I've taken Nessie out only twice in 40 years. It's time she saw more of my ugly mug. "

DEDICATION

66 When I think back now, I think I missed some of the fun out of life. Perhaps I was too dedicated. The laughs were there with the players but never away from the players. I was too serious. I lived the life of a monk and I carried it to extremes. 99

From Shanks – The Authorised Biography.

FRIENDSHIP

❝ I might add that I count Everton amongst the clubs who have welcomed me over the last few seasons. I have been received more warmly by Everton than I have been by Liverpool. ❞

From Shankly, his 1977 autobiography.

EARLY YEARS

" I don't think I was in a bath until I was 15 years old. I used to use a tub to wash myself. But out of poverty with a lot of people living in the same house, you get humour. **"**

SCOUSERS

" Although I'm a Scot, I'm proud to be called a Scouser. "

SAYING GOODBYE

" It was the most difficult thing in the world, when I went to tell
the chairman. It was like walking to the electric chair.
That's the way it felt. **"**

Deciding to leave the Liverpool job in 1974.

BIRTHDAYS

" Of course I didn't take my wife to see Rochdale as an anniversary present. It was her birthday. Would I have got married during the football season? Anyway, it was Rochdale reserves. **"**

Picture: *The Kop pays homage to Shankly in April 1973. (Peter Robinson/Empics)*

THE BEGINNING

" I make no promises except that I shall put everything into this job I have so willingly undertaken. **"**

After being appointed Liverpool manager, December 1959.

" Cricket? I'll give you cricket! **"**

Shankly visits Melwood for the first time, to be told that the best practice pitch was reserved for cricket.

THE REDS

66 Liverpool was made for me and I was made for Liverpool. 99

66 Chairman Mao has never seen a greater show of red
strength than today. 99

*Address to thousands of Liverpudlians gathered in the city to hail the
1974 FA Cup-winning team.*

INVINCIBILITY

" My idea was to build Liverpool into a bastion of invincibility.
Napoleon had that idea. He wanted to conquer the world.
I wanted Liverpool to be untouchable, to build the club
up and up until everyone would have to submit. **"**

❝ It's great grass at Anfield. Professional grass. **❞**

❝ This is to remind our lads who they're playing for, and to remind the opposition who they're playing against. **❞**

After the famous This Is Anfield plaque had been fixed above the players' tunnel.

THE RESERVES

❝ There are two great teams on Merseyside.
Liverpool and Liverpool Reserves. **❞**

THE KOP 1

“ I'm just one of the people who stand on the Kop.
They think the same as I do, and I think the same as they do.
It's a kind of marriage of people who like each other. **”**

“ Don't do that. That's someone's life. **”**

To a police officer who kicked a scarf thrown to Shankly from the Kop after Liverpool won the 1972/73 Championship.

THE RED SHIRT

" Fire in your belly comes from pride and passion in wearing the red shirt. We don't need to motivate players because each of them is responsible for the performance of the team as a whole. The status of Liverpool's players keeps them motivated. "

LIVERPOOL FC

❝ It's not a club, it's an institution and I wanted to bring the crowd closer to the club. People have their ashes scattered here. One family came when it was frosty and the groundsman dug a hole in the goal at the Kop end and inside the right-hand post a foot down there's a casket. Not only do they support Liverpool when they're alive, they do it when they're dead. This is why Liverpool are so great. There's no hypocrisy about it and that's how close people were brought to the club. It was sheer honesty, I brought them in, accepted them in. **❞**

Quoted in Shanks – The Authorised Biography.

A PEOPLE'S MAN

" I felt that the Liverpool people were my kind of people. What I achieved at Anfield I did for those fans. Together we turned Liverpool into one huge family, something alive and vibrant and warm and successful. I thank God for the people of Merseyside. The attitude of the people towards me and my family is stronger now than it ever was. I never cheated them and they never let me down. **"**

Quoted in the Liverpool Echo.

ROAD TO GLORY

" After the game, under the main stand at Anfield, I met three men from the Kop. On behalf of the Kop they presented me with a magnificent plaque entitled The Road To Glory, a complete record of my 15 years at Anfield. I also received a silver tankard engraved 'To Shanks, with thanks, a fan'. When I was going round the ground a teenager came out of the Kop and presented me with a greetings card more than two feet square. They had made it themselves, more than a thousand signatures on the card in red. I'll treasure these presents for the rest of my life because they come from people who mean everything to me. **"**

After Shankly's testimonial game at Anfield in 1975, quoted in the Liverpool Echo.

UNBEATABLE

" I want to build a team that's invincible, so they'll have to send a team from Mars to beat us. "

THE KOP 2

" When the ball is down the Kop end, they frighten the ball. Sometimes they suck it into the back of the net. **"**

" The Kop is exclusive, an institution, and if you're a member of the Kop, you feel you're a member of a society, you've got thousands of friends around you and they're united and loyal. **"**

" It was for the people of Liverpool and Liverpool FC. **"**

On his OBE.

THE END

“ I would like to be remembered first and foremost as a man who looked after his family. I would also like people to say that I created something through hard work and never cheated anybody… Above all I would like to be remembered as a man who was selfless, who strived and worried so that others could share the glory, and who built up a family of people who could hold their heads high and say, 'We are Liverpool'. ”

From Shankly, his autobiography.

...GRASS IN THE SKY

THE BOOK OF **CLOUGH**

Compiled by Alex Murphy

OLD BIG 'EAD IN HIS OWN WORDS

ISBN 0-9544177-2-0

> **❝** They say Rome wasn't built in a day, but I wasn't on that particular job. **❞**

> **❝** If God had wanted us to play football in the clouds, he'd have put grass in the sky. **❞**